Literary Hills of San Francisco

LITERARY
HILLS
OF
SAN
FRANCISCO

Luree Miller

STARRHILL PRESS
Washington & Philadelphia

For my children, Scott, Blair and Stacy,
who were born in the Bay Area

Starrhill Press, Inc., publisher
P.O. Box 32342
Washington, D.C. 20007
(202) 686-6703

Illustrations by Jonel Sofian.
Maps by Deb Norman.
Hand-marbled paper by Iris Nevins, Sussex, N.J.

Library of Congress Cataloging-in-Publication Data

Miller, Luree.
    Literary hills of San Francisco / Luree Miller. — 1st ed.
        p.   cm.
    Includes bibliographical references and index.
    ISBN 0-913515-76-0
    1. Literary landmarks—California—San Francisco. 2. Authors,
American—Homes and haunts—California—San Francisco. 3. American literature—California—San Francisco—History and criticism.
4. San Francisco (Calif.)—Description—Guide-books. 5. San
Francisco (Calif.)—Intellectual life.   I. Title.
PS144.S4M54 1992
810.9'979461—dc20
    [B]   91-44656
                                                                  CIP

Printed in the United States of America
First edition
9 8 7 6 5 4 3 2

Contents

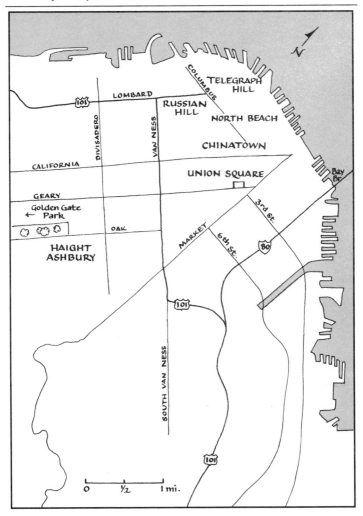

San Francisco

Literary Beginnings

San Francisco has always been one of my dream cities,
for it has the glamour of literature, without which
matter is a dead thing.

– Sir Arthur Conan Doyle

A "GOLD AND WHITE acropolis rising wave on wave against the
blue of the Pacific sky," is how John Steinbeck described San
Francisco, a city world famous for its visual glamour. Built on the
gold rush dreams of the forty-niners, it is a romantic upstart with a
short and dramatic history. In 1906, when San Francisco's toehold
on the edge of the continent had been established for only fifty
years, the earth under it suddenly shifted. The city slipped and
came crashing down in the greatest earthquake then known on the
North American continent.

In the aftermath of the quake, fires sprang up throughout the
city. For three days and two nights, thick red flames leapt unchecked
from house to house until more than five hundred city blocks
smoldered in ashes. A steady stream of people carrying their cats,
canaries, and parrots, their dogs trotting beside them, tramped
toward the safety of Golden Gate Park and the Presidio. Those San
Franciscans were philosophical, as were the residents of the city
eight decades later in 1988, when another earthquake struck.
Whatever disaster has shaken them, San Franciscans have always
rebuilt. Constant seismic threats do not daunt them. Sustained by
their dreams, they are optimistic survivors.

Only a few San Franciscan buildings cherished for literary
associations have survived earthquakes, fire and real estate development
as the city has grown, in little more than one hundred fifty years,

from a tent town to the sophisticated center of the sprawling metropolitan Bay Area.

Fortunately, however, the distinctive physical attributes of Conan Doyle's dream city remain unchanged. From every hill and bluff are spectacular views of sunlit, boat-filled San Francisco Bay, with the blue Pacific Ocean stretching to the far horizon. Soft, gray fog still wafts up suddenly over the cliffs and spreads down the streets. Moods change swiftly. The city becomes mysterious.

Great atmosphere is San Francisco's hallmark and a magnet for poets and authors. And the multicultural mix of friendly, informal, and tolerant San Franciscans adds to the attraction.

The walks I've chosen include some of the neighborhoods best-known for their literary associations, the few remaining houses where famous writers stayed and the plaques or streets commemorating them. But primarily these walks invite you to imbibe the intoxicating atmosphere of this ever-changing city, which has affected literary imaginations far out of proportion to its short history and small size. For San Francisco is small, as cities go, and eminently walkable.

Four of the five neighborhoods selected are so compact and close to each other that you can combine several walks at a brisker pace if time is short. The oldest section, Chinatown, Portsmouth Square and Jackson Square Historic District, is next door to Union Square. If you go west a few blocks on Columbus Avenue from Jackson Square Historic District, you'll be in North Beach, often called the Greenwich Village of the West, at the foot of Telegraph Hill. A few steep streets south of North Beach is Russian Hill, topped by a tiny park named for Ina Coolbrith, poet and muse, who amused Mark Twain and instructed Jack London.

These neighborhoods are the heart of San Francisco, intimately known to Robert Louis Stevenson, Mark Twain, Bret Harte, Ambrose Bierce, Jack London, Dashiell Hammett, William Saroyan,

Lawrence Ferlinghetti, Allen Ginsberg, Jack Kerouac, Alan Watts and others who found their atmosphere congenial to creativity and hung out here to hone their particular styles. This is the San Francisco eloquently extolled or excoriated by a continuing stream of visiting writers from Richard Henry Dana in 1835 through Anthony Trollope, Rudyard Kipling, Oscar Wilde, Arthur Conan Doyle, and Simone de Beauvoir, to Tom Wolfe and "gonzo" journalist Hunter S. Thompson.

Haight-Ashbury, on the edge of Golden Gate Park, was once the preserve of the affluent, who built big, beautifully decorated and turreted Victorian houses that still stand, interspersed among more middle-class ones. Haight-Ashbury was turbulent during the drug scene of the 1960s and 1970s, but now it is settling down to an interesting mixture of bohemianism and gentrification. Walking down Haight Street, with its funky shops, psychedelic signs and occasional aging flower children, evokes an era that began in San Francisco and rippled across America, causing a sea change in attitudes. "Hippie Hill," just inside Golden Gate Park, is an idyllic spot to sit and contemplate the counterculture that started here. Deeper in the park are the polo fields, where the great Human Be-In of 1967 was held.

Joan Didion, a sharp observer of the California scene, wrote about the Haight-Ashbury culture in her 1967 essay, "Slouching toward Bethlehem." And her earlier observation in "Notes from a Native Daughter" (1965) still holds true: "All that is constant about the California of my childhood is the rate at which it disappears."

RICHARD HENRY DANA was the first writer to note how quickly San Francisco grew. A Harvard man who went to sea as a common sailor, Dana later wrote an autobiographical account of his experiences in the classic, *Two Years before the Mast.* In the winter of 1835-36 Dana's Boston trading ship sailed along "the remote and almost unknown coast of California" and "floated into the vast solitude of the Bay of San Francisco." The

only other ship was a Russian brig, down from Sitka, the capital of
Russian Alaska, to winter in the bay. Dana observed a "ruinous"
Presidio or fort, and an "almost deserted" Mission Dolores, but,
he noted, "All around us was the stillness of nature."

Twenty-four years later, in 1859, Richard Dana returned to
San Francisco Bay and recorded his astonishment:

> We bore round the point toward the old anchoring-ground . . .
> and there, covering the sand-hills and the valleys, stretching
> from the water's edge to the base of the great hills, and from
> the Old Presidio to the Mission, flickering all over with the
> lamps of its streets and houses, lay a city of one hundred
> thousand inhabitants. Clipper ships of the largest size lay at
> anchor. When I reflected on what I once saw here, and what
> now surrounded me, I could scarcely keep my hold on reality
> at all, or the genuineness of anything, and seemed to myself
> like one who had moved in "worlds not realized."

The men and women who, a mere ten years earlier, flocked to
the gold fields in the great California Gold Rush of 1849 had built
this instant city that rose like a dream on the farthest edge of the
American frontier.

When the young, struggling Scot, **ROBERT LOUIS STEVEN-
SON,** came to San Francisco in 1879, a wonderful variety of ethnic
neighborhoods had already taken root. Stevenson was pursuing
Fanny Osbourne, a Californian he met and fell in love with in
France. While waiting for Fanny to obtain her divorce, the penniless
Stevenson prowled the streets. Later he would enjoy wealth and
fame from his much-loved books, *Treasure Island, Kidnapped,* and
Dr. Jekyll and Mr. Hyde. In Chinatown Stevenson wondered at the
"necromantic-looking vegetables," the "temple doors open and the
scent of the joss-stick streaming forth on the American air," "kites
of Oriental fashion hanging fouled in Western telegraph-wires." He
wandered through "Little Mexico, with its crazy wooden houses,
endless crazy wooden stairs," and in "Little Italy" he looked "at the
windows of small eating-shops, transported bodily from Genoa or

Naples, with their macaroni, and chianti flasks and portraits of Garibaldi."

The brash young **OSCAR WILDE** was beginning to make a name for himself when he arrived a few years later on his famous lecture tour of America. (Upon arriving at New York, Wilde told the customs official, "I have nothing to declare but my genius.") Wilde saw another side of San Francisco. The English aesthete (later the author of *The Importance of Being Earnest, Lady Windermere's Fan* and *The Picture of Dorian Gray*) checked in at the Palace Hotel, seven stories of luxury lavishly bolted with iron bands to withstand earthquakes. Its immense glass-roofed central court was furnished with potted palms, rocking chairs and spittoons and was bisected by a carriage driveway.

The young sports at the Bohemian Club and the old-timers at the Cliff House sized up this visiting tenderfoot poet in velvet knee breeches, with his dreaming eyes and languid manners, and decided to put him to the frontier tests of masculinity: drinking and poker. As night wore on at the Bohemian Club, Wilde matched his hosts drink for drink until they were all under the table, dead drunk. Then he rose, throwing his great cloak about him, to saunter back in the gray dawn to the Palace Hotel.

At the Cliff House, he was reluctantly drawn into a game of "dollar ante" by a bunch of knowing natives. The betting rose. Three aces were laid down, followed by a full house. Then, sighing deeply, Wilde delicately laid out his four deuces and reached for the money. "Now that I remember it, gentlemen," he murmured, "we used to indulge in this little recreation at Oxford." Or so the stories went.

RUDYARD KIPLING stayed at the same Palace Hotel a couple of years later, in 1889, on his way from India to England. In the Palm Court, he noted, "Most of the men wore frock-coats and top-hats—the things that we in India put on at a wedding breakfast if we possess them—but they all spat [into] spittoons of infinite capacity and generous gape."

By this time San Franciscans had demolished the hills that were too steep to grade and had sent cable cars up those that horses couldn't scale. The cable cars, Kipling observed, "turn corners almost at right angles; cross other lines, and, for aught I know, may run up the sides of houses." San Francisco, he concluded, "is a mad city— inhabited for the most part by perfectly insane people whose women are of a remarkable beauty."

Writing home to his Aunt Georgy, Kipling assured her that he had found her friend Mrs. Carr, who was living in a "funny little house all of painted wood (which is the custom in Frisco). I am to give you all her love and tell you that America has hardened her and she can now watch a street accident or a shooting affray without any emotion!"

Such insouciance served its citizens well when the great earthquake of 1906 struck. **ALICE B. TOKLAS,** who was born and raised in the city, wrote in her memoir, *What Is Remembered:*

> Life went on calmly until one morning we and our home were
> violently shaken by an earthquake. Gas was escaping. I hurried
> to my father's bedroom, pulled up the shades, pulled back the
> curtains and opened the windows. My father was apparently
> asleep. Do get up, I said to him. The city is on fire. That, said
> he with his usual calm, will give us a black eye in the East.

Toklas walked up the hill to the Presidio, and her father, finally risen, "walked down to the business quarter to see if the vaults of his bank were holding."

ALICE B. TOKLAS, ROBERT FROST, ISADORA DUNCAN and **SHIRLEY JACKSON** were among the native-born on whom the city made little lasting impression. Toklas and Duncan went to Europe. Jackson settled in Vermont. Her stories and novels appeared in the 1950s and 1960s and include "The Lottery," her famous tale of a murdered scapegoat in a small town. Frost left when he was eleven and also became a New Englander. Four-time winner of the Pulitzer Prize for poetry, he penned a few evocative lines about his western childhood in the 1870s and 1880s in "West-Running Brook":

> Dust always blowing about the town,
> Except when sea-fog laid it down,
> And I was one of the children told
> Some of the blowing dust was gold.

That there was something unique in the air of San Francisco **SIR ARTHUR CONAN DOYLE** perceived when he stopped over in 1923 to deliver several lectures. The world-famous creator of Sherlock Holmes was also conducting some psychic research, a pursuit that occupied the last years of his life. Doyle declared that this city built on hills stood "first in natural beauty of all the cities in the world," but concluded sadly, "On closer acquaintance I have found San Francisco far less psychic than Los Angeles."

San Franciscans argue emphatically that their city is *totally* different from Los Angeles and, for that matter, any other American city. Perched on the Pacific Rim, San Francisco, more than any other western metropolis, looks west to the East. Writers seeking enlightenment or adventure and feeling that Eastern pull have sailed forth from the Golden Gate: **ROBERT LOUIS STEVENSON** to Samoa, **MARK TWAIN** to the Sandwich (Hawaiian) Islands, **JACK LONDON** to Korea and **GARY SNYDER** to Japan. Those staying in the city who were attracted to Oriental philosophies found local Zen masters or Tibetan Buddhist monks to gather around. From the beginning, San Francisco has had a strong Asian presence, at first separate and exotic, but increasingly accessible as a growing number of gifted Asian-American writers such as **MAXINE HONG KINGSTON, GUS LEE** and **AMY TAN** give voice to the Oriental worlds within the city.

Other ethnic areas that attract writers and add richness to San Francisco's cosmopolitan character, like the Latino Mission district and the largely black Fillmore, are left out of this book because they have fewer landmarks and the distances between them are greater.

San Francisco writers walk their beloved streets for inspiration. As you explore you might catch a glimpse of such literary residents as feminist writer **TILLIE OLSEN** (*Tell Me a Riddle*) or novelist

ERNEST J. GAINES (his fictional *Autobiography of Miss Jane Pittman* is a saga of black history), Pulitzer Prize-winning **ALICE WALKER** (*The Color Purple*) or **MAYA ANGELOU**, who described why she, at thirteen, felt "intoxicated by the physical fact of San Francisco" in *I Know Why the Caged Bird Sings.* The brightest literary stars currently shining in the San Francisco firmament are women and members of minority groups.

A bit removed and aloof from the intensity of these throbbing sections is the dreamlike elegance of Pacific Heights, where best-selling writer **DANIELLE STEELE** lives in a forty-two-room mansion. It, too, is a wonderful place to walk. Gawk at the marvelous array of gardens and houses, and revel in the stunning views of the ocean, the bay and both the Golden Gate and Bay bridges. If you sit awhile in lovely Lafayette Park, with its plaque honoring recently rediscovered California novelist **GERTRUDE ATHERTON**, you'll see a more colorful cross section of residents than lived here at the turn of the century, when only the very rich could afford this location. You might spot some bohemian or yuppie characters who live nearby, like those portrayed in the novel *Caroline's Daughters* by the much-acclaimed contemporary resident of San Francisco, **ALICE ADAMS**. Bus service is excellent all over the city, and visitors with time can explore these areas.

Market Street, beginning at the Ferry Building, one of San Francisco's most venerable landmarks, is the main artery and diagonal division line of the city. Streets northwest of Market run north-south or east-west. Streets southeast of Market run parallel or at right angles to Market. The plan looks like two neat checker-boards made by people who couldn't agree where north was. Within both parts, hills make occasional disruptions. Some streets stop abruptly at the edge of a precipitous hill, then reappear at a lower level or on the other side. For all of the straight corridors cutting through the city, like California, Columbus, and Market, there are many footlanes, alleys and little streets that dead-end or double back upon themselves: they are unmarked on most maps. And one of the most delightful and distinctive features of San Francisco are the connecting stairways down hills and between streets. Some, still wooden and almost hidden by lush hillside gardens, help us to imagine what the city was like before the advent of cable cars, when the only way up or down a steep hill was by stairway. Whenever possible, I've planned the walks so that you can take a bus or cable car to the top of a hill and walk down a stairway.

To find out how to get by public transportation from where you are to where a walk begins, and from the walk's end back again, call: 673-MUNI or 673-6864. At the top of the page of directions for each walk, I have noted the intersection where the walk begins and where it ends. Few taxis cruise the streets beyond the downtown area.

The only writers' homes in the Bay Area that have been turned into public museums are those of **JACK LONDON, JOHN MUIR** and **EUGENE O'NEILL**. Each house is an easy half-day or day trip across the bay from San Francisco. Driving across the 1¾-mile-long Golden Gate Bridge or the 8¼-mile-long San Francisco-Oakland Bay Bridge is part of the San Francisco experience. Notes on each of these writers houses are at the back of the book.

Chinatown

Chinatown, Portsmouth Square and Jackson Square

> The birds, and the flowers, and the Chinamen, and the winds, and the sunshine, and all things that go to make life happy, are present in San Francisco today, just as they are all days in the year.
>
> *– Mark Twain*

MARK TWAIN, the first great American writer to thumb his nose at the European literary tradition, honed his distinctly American frontier style by writing for San Francisco newspapers and literary magazines. In the oldest section of the city, where Twain lived and wrote, frequented saloons and ate in Chinese restaurants, the polyglot population quickened his imagination and sharpened his ear. "There is no such thing as 'the Queen's English,' " he wrote. "The property has gone into the hands of a joint stock company and we own the bulk of the shares."

Walk down Grant Avenue into Chinatown now and you will hear an even more astonishing babel than Twain heard. Originally settled largely by Cantonese, Chinatown now is bursting with ethnic Chinese from Vietnam, Laos, Burma, Thailand, Malaysia and Hong Kong, each group with its own dialect. Some of these new Americans will no doubt enrich the expanding Asian-American literary heritage that was pioneered by writers like **JADE SNOW WONG.** The daughter of poor immigrants from imperial China, Wong wrote a 1950 surprise best-seller, *Fifth Chinese Daughter*, about growing up in Chinatown.

Chinatown has always been a city within a city. It is the largest settlement of Chinese in the world outside of China. Here tradition reigns: Buddhist temples top ornate old buildings with brightly painted yellow, red and green balconies, dragons curl up lampposts, and bins of exotic Chinese edibles spill out onto the street from tiny aromatic markets. Small wonder that mystery writers like Dashiell Hammett, Erle Stanley Gardner and a legion of pulp writers succumbed to set pieces about the mysterious East and laid their chases through the labyrinth of these crowded streets, alleys and buildings. Writing as outsiders holding the racist attitudes of their times, they peopled Chinatown with stereotypical Fu Manchu-like villains.

For a writer to depict family and community life centered around such venerable institutions as St. Mary's Catholic Church, built in the 1850s on granite foundations shipped from China, would shatter readers' assumptions about the sinister inscrutability of Orientals. So when the twenty-four-year-old Jade Snow Wong, who noted that she "had spent half of her life working and living, without romance, in a Chinatown basement," wrote her triumphant story, it was a revelation. Told in the ancient Chinese literary form using the third person singular, "reflecting cultural disregard for the individual," its author was most unlikely: a Chinese woman brought up with strict nineteenth-century Chinese standards, who, when "corresponding with an older person like my father, would write, in words half the size of the regular ideographs, 'small daughter Jade Snow.' " Hers was a new view from the inside looking out.

As the Asian-American viewpoint enlarged, less sanguine writers like militant **FRANK CHIN**, author of *The Chickencoop Chinaman* and *Donald Duk*, saw Chinatown in the 1950s and 1960s as a stifling ghetto. And feminist writers, in memoirs recounting legends and tales told by their Chinese mothers, struggled for insight into the dual, conflicting identities of Chinese Americans: **MAXINE HONG KINGSTON** in *The Woman Warrior* (1975) and **AMY TAN** in *The Joy Luck Club* (1989). Kingston and Tan are stunning new writers who quickly won literary acclaim and commercial success. Kingston followed with *The Tripmaster Monkey* (1989) and Tan with *The Kitchen God's Wife* (1991). Another highly successful Asian-American writer is **GUS LEE**, with his heart-warming semi-autobiographical novel, *China Boy* (1991), set in a predominantly black San Francisco neighborhood.

Tourists throng along Grant Avenue, the city's oldest street, and Stockton has become the main shopping street for the community. But on both streets you can feel the vitality that makes Chinatown thrive.

A small wall plaque between 823 and 837 Grant Avenue commemorates the site of the first habitation in San Francisco. An English sea captain named William Richardson put up a tent here in 1835, then built a rough board shanty. Richardson was the "solitary settler" Richard Henry Dana described in *Two Years Before the Mast*. However, Chinese immigrants soon claimed the area and, after the 1906 earthquake, rebuilt it so quickly that they foiled the city fathers' plans to move them off this prime piece of property.

The three-tiered pagoda at Grant and Washington, once the Old Chinese Telephone Exchange and now a branch of the Bank of Canton, is on the site where San Francisco's first newspaper, the *California Star*, was published. Its story headlined "Gold!" was picked up by the *New York Herald* in August 1848 and helped spark the great gold stampede that year.

By that time Portsmouth Square, just a few steps down Washington Street, had become the center of town. Here, in 1879, the tubercular **ROBERT LOUIS STEVENSON** whiled away his days on a bench writing and dreaming of his love, Fanny Osbourne, a Californian whom he had met in France. That year his small classic, *Travels with a Donkey in the Cevennes*, was published, but he was penniless. The next year Fanny's divorce was final, and they married and returned to Stevenson's Scotland.

Stevenson became rich and famous with his adventure books. When he revisited America nine years later, editors and publishers met him in New York and offered lucrative contracts. But in San Francisco he had to overcome the suspicion that writers were poor business risks before he was able to charter the yacht on which he and Fanny sailed out of the Golden Gate to the South Seas, never to return. They settled in Samoa, where Stevenson died at the age of forty-four.

A monument to Stevenson erected by his friends stands in the southwest corner of Portsmouth Square. Inscribed with an excerpt from his *Christmas Sermon*, it is crowned with a model of the galleon *Hispaniola* from *Treasure Island* in full sail. Nearby, Chinese men sun on the benches or gather in the outdoor game room in the opposite corner of the square; children climb on a modern toy dragon, and a bridge from the square leads to the Chinese Cultural Center in the Holiday Inn, where there are exhibits and information for tours of Chinatown.

Rough, exuberant, affluent early San Francisco sprouted newspapers and literary journals faster than any other city on the North American continent. Since news from the East Coast arrived infrequently and irregularly, by overland stagecoach or pony express or from ships coming around Cape Horn, citizens depended on local papers and literary journals to inform and entertain them. By the mid-1850s San Francisco boasted that it published more newspapers than London and more books than all the rest of the land west of the Mississippi combined. By the midsixties four newspapers had been established: the San Francisco *Examiner, Chronicle, Call-Bulletin* and *News*. The city supported all four for nearly a century. Periodicals and newspapers in Chinese, Japanese, Italian, Spanish, Russian, French, German, Greek, Portuguese and Yiddish sprang up.

In 1869 the transcontinental railroad was completed, ending the city's isolation, and San Franciscans went on a three-day spree. But the city's character was set: San Francisco was a literary town—a western proving ground for innovators from Mark Twain, Bret Harte and Jack London to William Saroyan, Allen Ginsberg and Amy Tan.

The Montgomery Block, the city's first fireproof building, was built in 1853 on a raft of redwood trees and withstood the 1906 earthquake and fire. Affectionately known as the "Monkey Block," it was the most enduring and important city literary landmark until it was pulled down more than a century later in 1959. Now replaced by the Transamerica Building, a modern Eiffel Tower-like symbol of San Francisco, the "Monkey Block" is still mourned by literary aficionados for its association with writers like Robert Louis Stevenson, Bret Harte, Mark Twain, Ambrose Bierce and Jack London, as well as the writers, artists and revolutionaries of the 1930s and 1940s.

A building with commercial establishments on the street level and three floors of high-ceilinged, big-windowed rooms above, the "Monkey Block" became the hangout of painters, poets, musicians, journalists and freelance writers when the tonier law firms, stockbrokers and mining companies moved farther down Montgomery Street. Here Sun Yat-sen sat in a former law office in the early 1900s, plotting the overthrow of the Manchu Dynasty and writing a new constitution for China. But even after the establishment tenants left, the sumptuous Bank Exchange bar in the Montgomery Building, with its white marble floor, stayed in business, and many a famous elbow was bent beneath its chandeliers.

One of the earliest was **MARK TWAIN**'s. He contemplated the painting of Samson and Delilah hanging behind the bar, which was said to be a valuable import from Europe. It was a perfect foil for the down-home frontier storytelling style the twenty-eight-year-old Twain was hearing all around him and transforming into his own inimitable voice. In the weekly *Golden Era* he wrote:

> You take a stranger into the Bank Exchange and show him the magnificent picture of Samson and Delilah, and what is the first object he notices? —Samson's fine face and flaming eye? or the noble beauty of his form? or the lovely, half-nude Delilah? or the muscular Philistine behind Samson, who is furtively admiring her charms? —or the perfectly counterfeited folds of the rich drapery below her knees? or the symmetry and truth to nature of Samson's left foot? No, sir, the first thing that catches his eye is the scissors on the floor at Delilah's feet, and the first thing he says, "Them scissors is too modern—there warn't no scissors like that in them days, by a d—d sight!"

In the Montgomery Block Turkish Baths, Mark Twain often played penny ante with a man named Tom Sawyer. Then Twain might stroll over to the offices of the *Golden Era* at 732 Montgomery Street to join a group of young writers, known as the Bohemians, who met there.

Under his birth name, Samuel Clemens, Twain had served in the Confederate Army for a few disillusioning weeks in early 1861 and then jumped at the chance to go west with his brother Orion, who had been appointed territorial secretary for Nevada Territory. Clemens didn't find the gold or silver he had hoped for, but he discovered in the Far West that he could write. Soon he was commuting across the Sierra Nevada Mountains to San Francisco. By 1863 he had adopted his pen name, a river-sounding call from his days on the Mississippi as a steamboat captain: *mark twain* means "two fathoms deep."

Twain moved to San Francisco the next year. In the Jackson Square Historic District one can imagine his distinctive figure, with its careless slouch, rumpled suit and unruly mop of auburn hair, ambling up the street to meet his journalist colleagues at one of the many saloons and stopping to talk with everyone he met along the way. "It is like being in Hannibal [Missouri] and meeting the old familiar faces," he wrote his mother. "I fare like a prince wherever I go, be it on this side of the mountains or the other."

BRET HARTE, already an established literary figure, became Twain's mentor, critiquing his manuscripts and teaching him grammar. Harte, elegant to the point of dandyism, was Twain's opposite in appearance and style. But they were close friends.

The social satirist in Twain found plenty of scope in free-wheeling San Francisco. He lampooned Bay Area speculators and the local police so effectively that he thought it prudent to leave town for a couple of months. Back in a Nevada mining camp he heard a yarn about a jumping frog that he jotted in his notebook. A year later, in 1865, "The Celebrated Jumping Frog of Calaveras County" appeared in an eastern paper, and overnight everyone was talking about Mark Twain. His persona as a shrewd western humorist and a teller of tall tales was established, and the public, in rebellion against proper Bostonian standards, was ready to listen.

On a newspaper assignment to the Sandwich Islands, Twain developed the art of writing travel reports. When the *Alta California* sent him to Europe and the Holy Land to write travel pieces, he "bade good-bye to the friendliest land and liveliest, heartiest community on our continent," and "after seven years of vicissitudes, ended a 'pleasure trip' to the silver mines of Nevada which had originally been intended to occupy only three months." Those travel articles established Twain's reputation when he later assembled them in his sensationally successful book, *The Innocents Abroad.*

All of Mark Twain's books, the critic Bernard DeVoto observed, "are embryonic in what he had written by December, 1866, when he went east. These casual pieces outline the future: the humorist, the social satirist, the pessimist, the novelist of America, Mark Twain exhilarated, sentimental, cynical, angry, and depressed, all are here. The rest is only development." San Francisco, as well as Hannibal, Missouri, can rightly claim the first great authentic American writer as its own.

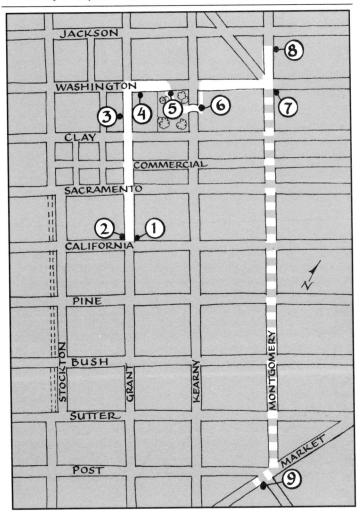

Chinatown / Portsmouth Square / Jackson Square

Walk 1: Chinatown, Portsmouth Square and Jackson Square Historic District

Begin at California and Grant Avenue. End at Montgomery and Columbus Avenue or Montgomery and Market.

Old St. Mary's Catholic Church (1) on the northeast corner of California and Grant was built on a foundation of granite shipped from China in the 1850s.

On the northwest corner is the **Chinatown Wax Museum (2)** with life-size wax figures depicting events in Chinese-American history. Open daily. Admissions charge.

Walk into Chinatown along Grant Avenue. Between Nos. 832 and 837 is a **plaque (3)** commemorating the first habitation built in San Francisco, in 1837, by English sea captain William Richardson.

Turn right on Washington Street to the **Bank of Canton (4)** at 743. Built in the style of a northern Chinese pagoda, this was the Old Chinese Telephone Exchange. Step inside the bank to hear the sound of modern Chinese. A plaque on the threshold just to the right of the entrance commemorates the *California Star*, San Francisco's first newspaper, which in 1848 scooped the discovery of gold.

Continue down Washington Street. A few steps into Portsmouth Square is a **monument to Robert Louis Stevenson (5)** topped by the galleon *Hispaniola*, which is immortalized in *Treasure Island*.

From Portsmouth Square, cross the footbridge to the **Chinese Cultural Center (6)** in the Holiday Inn. Here the nonprofit Chinese Cultural Foundation offers exhibits and programs, and you may sign up for a Chinese Heritage Walk through Chinatown, on Saturdays only, unless advance arrangements are made. Tel: 415-986-1822.

Take the Holiday Inn elevator to ground level and exit back on Washington Street. Continue east downhill one block to the pyramid-shaped **Transamerica Building (7)** looming skyward on the site of the old four-storied Montgomery Block. The "Monkey

Block" stood from 1853 until 1959, an earthquake survivor and center for literary figures, including Robert Louis Stevenson, Bret Harte, Mark Twain, Ambrose Bierce, Jack London and many others.

Here Washington Street, Columbus Avenue (which leads to North Beach) and Montgomery Street converge. Turn left and go north on Montgomery Street into the Jackson Square Historic District. **730–732 Montgomery Street (8)** housed the *Golden Era* from 1852 to 1856, a weekly that published fledgling writers like Bret Harte and Mark Twain who met at its offices.

Return along Montgomery Street to Washington Street and enter the Redwood Grove Park behind the Transamerica Building. Here is an oasis of quiet, with California redwood trees, benches, and an adjoining restaurant and small foot passage with snack bars. From here you can return through Chinatown to your starting point.

Optional: A brisk ten-minute walk from Jackson Square Historic District south on Montgomery Street, through a canyon of tall office and bank buildings (Wells Fargo Bank has a stagecoach in its window), will bring you to the historic **Palace Hotel (9)**, newly restored, with its famous Garden Court, where reservations are needed for lunch or dinner.

Walking time is under an hour, exclusive of shopping or exploring in Chinatown and Jackson Square Historic District. In Jackson Square most shops are wholesale; the few that aren't display a retail sign.

Union Square / Downtown

California, more than any other part of the Union, is a
country by itself, and San Francisco a capital.
                                                – James Bryce

SINCE PIONEER DAYS, Union Square has been the center of
San Francisco. Public meetings to support the Union side in
the Civil War were held here in the 1860s. In the 1960s flower
children floated their balloons and flaunted their counterculture.
Whatever social issue dominates the city's life finds expression
in Union Square.

Department stores, swank shops and the historic St. Francis
Hotel surround the square. But just a few blocks behind the modern
facades lies the old San Francisco, where four- and five-story apartment
buildings are fronted with ironwork balconies connected by fire-
escape stairs. Every second-story balcony has a hand crank to wind
down the last ladder to the street. Lace curtains drape bow windows.
Brick walls border dead-end alleys. This area is detective writer
DASHIELL HAMMETT's beat.

Sam Spade, Hammett's fictional hard-boiled detective,
shadowed these streets in his trademark trench coat and created
a romantic gloss for pre-World War II San Francisco as Sherlock
Holmes had done for Victorian London. Humphrey Bogart played
Spade in John Huston's classic film version of *The Maltese Falcon*
(1930). Hammett fans know every site in the city described in
the writer's short stories and novels, and specialized walking tours
point them out. One of the most famous spots, from *The
Maltese Falcon*, is in Burritt Alley off Bush Street. A bronze
plaque states: "On approximately this spot Miles Archer, partner

of Sam Spade, was done in by Brigid O'Shaughnessy." Hammett's *Thin Man* (1932) was also made into a highly successful movie starring William Powell and Myrna Loy.

Dashiell Hammett was born and raised in the East, where, he said, there were "square houses, circle lives." He had traveled throughout the United States as a detective for the Pinkerton National Detective Agency, and he preferred the West. Shortly after he married and settled in San Francisco, his recurring tuberculosis forced him to quit the agency. Broke and desperate, Hammett decided to try writing detective stories. The ones he read seemed ridiculous. He *knew* the life. He became the acknowledged founder of the hard-boiled school of detective writing.

His biographer, Diane Johnson, notes that before Hammett was thirty he was so ill that "he would creep across the room to the bathroom only by holding on to a row of chairs that he had lined up for the purpose. But he kept on writing."

Because of his tuberculosis, Hammett's wife, Jose, set up a separate household with their two daughters across the bay, and Hammett lived alone in a series of apartments in the city. He visited his family on weekends and once wrote Jose, "I got back home safe and practically sober." His drinking was increasing.

The Maltese Falcon, which Hammett wrote while living at No. 891 Post Street and dedicated to Jose, catapulted him to success. The same year, 1930, he met Lillian Hellman, playwright and novelist, who wrote that "Dash" at that time was "the hottest thing in Hollywood and New York." Their stormy romance, which lasted until his death in 1961, became legendary, and Hammett never returned to live in the city that inspired his finest writing.

Established in 1872 as a social club for journalists, the Bohemian Club soon admitted (male only) artists and writers, including Bret Harte, George Sterling, Ambrose Bierce, Joaquin Miller, John Muir and Jack London. In the 1880s the club bought land covered with redwood trees on the Russian River and dubbed it the Bohemian Grove. Members retreated there annually to frolic and rededicate themselves to the Spirit of Bohemia with poetry, pageants and plays they had written. The poet **GEORGE STERLING** wrote, in 1907, a celebrated verse drama, *The Triumph of Bohemia*, in which Mammon is slain. But today's membership consists mainly of rich and powerful white men.

On the Post Street side of the Bohemian Club's building is a large bas-relief plaque depicting the colorful pioneer characters created by **BRET HARTE.** Bret Harte came to California in 1854, a slender seventeen-year-old with curly black hair, a mustache and an aquiline nose. He wore patent leather shoes, carried a morocco dressing case, and was not very practical. He did a bit of tutoring, wrote sentimental verses, drifted to the mining towns and back again, and finally landed a steady job as a printer's devil on a weekly paper in Union (now Arcata) on the northern coast of California. Soon he was gathering news and writing leaders.

At a fateful moment, during the editor's brief absence, Harte was left in charge of the paper. Abruptly the ugly underside of frontier life confronted him. At four in the morning of February 26, 1860, a gang of local riffraff without provocation murdered sixty Indians, mostly women and children, with hatchets and axes.

Harte was sickened and outraged. He headlined his scathing condemnation of the mob: "Indiscriminate Massacre of Indians— Women and Children Butchered." Harte's views suddenly put him in a dangerously unpopular position with the townspeople. Shortly after his story appeared, he sailed for San Francisco.

Beginning again as a typesetter on *The Golden Era*, Harte wrote prolifically, but no more sentimental verses. In 1868, he was appointed founding editor of the *Overland Monthly*, a literary journal that quickly reached eastern readers. The second issue carried Harte's story, "The Luck of Roaring Camp," followed soon after by "The Outcasts of Poker Flat" and "Tennessee's Partner." Overnight he was a literary sensation.

Lured East, Harte left San Francisco in 1871. Never able to match the success of his California stories, he eventually exiled himself to Europe. But his place in American literature is firmly established as the creator of a new Western genre of short story and a new movement—the local-color school.

In 1868, the same year that Harte shot to fame, **AMBROSE BIERCE** began writing a sardonic, often scathing, column attacking "folly, cant, hypocrisy and villainy in the persons of their representatives." It ran in various San Francisco journals for the next thirty years. Member of the Bohemian Club and friend of Bret Harte and Mark Twain, Bierce is best remembered for his satiric *Devil's Dictionary* (1906) and for his legendary disappearance across the border into Mexico to join Pancho Villa's army in 1913. At seventy-one he wrote, "To be a Gringo in Mexico—ah, that is Euthanasia."

Carlos Fuentes based his 1985 novel, *The Old Gringo*, on the Bierce legend, and Jane Fonda made a highly romantic film of it with Gregory Peck starring as Ambrose Bierce.

The **Press Club** of San Francisco claims to be the oldest organization of its kind on the continent. Efforts to organize began in congenial bars, and a constitution was finally written in 1888. "Tombstone," the symbol of the club, was a black cat that, according to legend, dozed on the club's hearth. The club was destroyed in the great earthquake and fire of 1906, but when the rubble cooled, the faithful black cat was found curled on the remaining doorstep, snoozing in the sun. "Tombstone" can be seen in the plaque by the Press Club door.

Contemporary columnist **HERB CAEN,** who has been carrying on a long love affair with the city in his columns and books, including *Only in San Francisco* (1960), claims that San Francisco is a newspaperman's town and fondly remembers when the old Press Club, with slot machines in the bar, stayed open all night.

ISADORA DUNCAN, great revolutionary of dance and daughter of California pioneers, was born on Taylor Street in 1878. Isadora Duncan's theories of dance blend classic forms with Walt Whitman's aesthetic of free expression. "I am indeed the spiritual daughter of Walt Whitman," she wrote. Isadora was directed in her early reading by California's first poet laureate, Ina Coolbrith (who also guided Jack London). She married the great Russian poet, Sergei Essenin, in 1922, but the marriage lasted only a year.

Breaking with tradition, Isadora danced barefoot, wearing loose Greek tunics and long scarves. One of her scarves, worn offstage, caused her tragic death in France in 1927. As she rode in an open-topped car, it caught in the wheel and strangled her.

The same year, her autobiography, *My Life*, appeared. John Dos Passos gave Isadora a biographical sketch in his novel, *The Big Money*. *Your Isadora*, is a collection of her letters to stage-designer Gordon Craig, with whom she had an ill-fated affair. *Isadora Speaks* contains her writings and talks. "The Dancer of the future," she declared, "shall dance the freedom of women."

The present **St. Francis Hotel** is built on its original 1903 steel skeleton frame, which withstood the great earthquake and fire of 1906. This grand old hotel is justly proud of its long prominence and is still a favored setting for literary meetings, real and fictional.

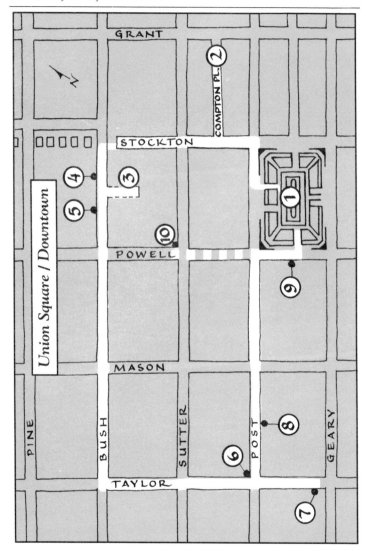

Walk 2: Union Square / Downtown

Begin at Union Square.
End at Union Square.

Union Square (1) is surrounded by shops, restaurants, department stores and hotels. But a few blocks away are three- and four-storied buildings with bay windows, decorated fronts, iron fire escapes and balconies. It's Dashiell Hammett atmosphere with turn-of-the-century to pre-World War II architecture. Exit Union Square at the corner of Post and Stockton streets.

Walk north a half block on Stockton Street and peer down **Compton Place (2),** typical of narrow lanes favored by San Francisco detective writers. At the end of Compton Place is the site of Temple Bar, a long-established restaurant frequented by writers and said to be the favorite of Ambrose Bierce, a "literary lion" of the 1880s.

Continue on Stockton Street, climb the left side of the Stockton Street stairs to Bush Street and turn left. At **Burritt Alley (3)** is a plaque commemorating Sam Spade, Dashiell Hammett's fictional detective. Across the street at **608 Bush (4)** is a plaque honoring Robert Louis Stevenson. Close by is **Dashiell Hammett Lane (5).**

Continue west on Bush Street. At Taylor Street, turn left downhill. At the corner of Taylor and Post is the **Bohemian Club (6)**. On the Post Street side of the club is a plaque commemorating Bret Harte with bas-relief figures of his most famous characters.

Continue south on Taylor Street. On the west side of the street between Post and Geary is a lane named for Isadora Duncan. In the same block, at **601 Taylor (7)**, near the corner of Geary, is the site of Isadora Duncan's birthplace and a plaque in her honor.

Return to Post Street. Turn right and walk east past the **Press Club (8)** at 555 Post with its symbol, the black cat "Tombstone," at its entrance.

Turn right on Powell Street to the historic **St. Francis Hotel (9)** opposite Union Square.

Optional: At the corner of Sutter and Powell is the **Holiday Inn at Union Square (10)** (it is really a block from the square). On the thirtieth floor, with spectacular views, is the Sherlock Holmes Public House and Drinking Salon with Victorian decor, Holmes memorabilia and a glassed-in replica of Holmes's sitting rooms at 221B Baker Street.

This walk takes approximately one-half hour.

"Tombstone,"
the Press Club's black cat

Telegraph Hill and North Beach

Telegraph Hill is a miniature Montmartre.
— *Simone de Beauvoir*

KNOWN AS the bohemian quarter of the city, Telegraph Hill and North Beach have always attracted the adventurous. In the 1850s the hill was dotted with little taverns with Dickensian names like "The Boar's Head," "The Magpie" and "The Jolly Waterman," where unwary visitors ran the risk of being sandbagged and frisked. A citizen's vigilante committee cleaned out the unsavory offenders by the 1860s, and writers and artists began moving in. But there were other intruders: Bret Harte complained about the wild goats eating the geraniums in his second-story windows and thumping across his roof at night "like heavy hailstones." Among other writers who lived on Telegraph Hill were Mark Twain, Joaquin Miller, Frank Norris and Ambrose Bierce. "The days of high revelry among the cabins and shanties of Telegraph Hill are wonderful to remember," wrote Kathleen Norris in *My San Francisco* (1915).

Today an abundance of alleys, lanes and stairways overgrown with rhododendrons and roses still suggests secret passageways and clandestine rendezvous. Flat-roofed buildings tiered down to the blue Pacific, wisteria tumbling over the walls, and breezes scented by lemon and eucalyptus trees lend an aura of Mediterranean glamour. And a host of fictional characters, as well as artists and writers, have climbed the wooden stairways to refresh their spirits with the stunning views and romantic ambience.

ROBERT LOUIS STEVENSON, in 1880, according to a popular legend, paused on his climb up the hill to rest fortuitously in front of the home of poet and author CHARLES WARREN STODDARD, who later became secretary for Mark Twain in London. Stoddard invited Stevenson into his hillside aerie to show him his collection of "strange objects," as Stevenson later described them in his novel *The Wrecker*. They were primitive artifacts, stone images and shell ornaments that Stoddard had collected on his travels in the South Seas. The two men became great friends and Stoddard gave Stevenson a copy of his *South-Sea Idylls*, which planted the seed for Stevenson's later exile to Samoa.

For about a century, writers living on the far edge of affluence found the cheap rents for the little wooden cottages, originally built by fishermen, worth the climb up the hill. Even recently, beginning writers might be lucky enough to find modest digs here, as did novelists Richard Brautigan and Armistead Maupin. But now almost all of the quaint houses' interiors have been expensively renovated, and Telegraph Hill is a sought-after address for businessmen and lawyers.

But North Beach, with its rich mix of ethnic restaurants and coffeehouses where writers still gather, clings to its Greenwich Village atmosphere. The "Beat Generation," claiming it as their turf, focused national attention on North Beach in the 1950s, and a counterculture lives on in the publications and avant-garde events sponsored by the City Lights Bookstore.

IRVING STONE, JACK LONDON's biographer (*Sailor on Horseback*), was born in 1903 on Washington Square at the foot of Telegraph Hill in the same year that London's classic *Call of the Wild* was published. Although London was also born in San Francisco (in 1876), he grew up in Oakland, across the bay. INA COOLBRITH, San Francisco poet and colleague of the Mark Twain-Bret Harte bunch, worked in the Oakland Public Library during London's youth, and London credited her with encouraging and directing his omnivorous reading.

London was America's first working-class writer and a self-proclaimed son of the West. Handsome and daring, he had an enormous capacity for work, both physical and intellectual. As a common laborer he worked sixteen-hour days, and he wrote fifty volumes of short stories, essays, and novels in his short life.

London achieved a worldwide fame that endures in the many translations of his best works, including *The Sea Wolf* (1904), *White Fang* (1906) and *The Valley of the Moon* (1913), as well as *The Call of the Wild*. He was an intense man, hard drinking, an ardent socialist and reckless adventurer. In the time-honored tradition of taking to the road for both adventure and material, Jack London rode the rails across America, went to sea, and followed the gold rush north in 1897 to the Klondike. The Klondike log cabin he lived in during his unsuccessful year of prospecting is on display at Jack London Square on Oakland's waterfront.

Jack London knew the San Francisco waterfront, too—he once worked as an oyster pirate—and the bars of North Beach. With emotions eerily similar to those of the Beat Generation bent on drug-induced self-destruction, London recounts, in his autobiographical novel, *John Barleycorn* (1913), how one night, after a three-week binge, he fell, dead drunk, into San Francisco Bay:

> Some maundering fancy of going out with the tide suddenly obsessed me. . . . Thoughts of suicide had never entered my head. And now that they entered, I thought it fine, a splendid culmination, a perfect rounding off of my short but exciting career. . . . John Barleycorn, laying me by the heels of my imagination and in a drug-dream [was] dragging me to death.

He floated out with the tide, singing to the stars. Then in a sudden terror of sobriety, he struggled out of his clothes and tried to swim. As daylight broke, a Greek fisherman hauled him in, unconscious, over the side of his boat, saving his life.

For many years afterward, Jack London stayed away from wild drinking parties. In 1907 he and his second wife Charmain, his "Mate-Woman," set sail in their boat, "The Snark," for an extended voyage in the South Pacific. In 1911 they moved to Glen Ellen in

Sonoma County, where in 1916 London died, burned out, at the age of forty.

Another Oakland writer who frequented San Francisco and knew Ina Coolbrith was the flamboyant poet **JOAQUIN MILLER** . Bret Harte, as editor of the *Overland Monthly*, rejected Miller's poetry, and so did other publishers. Coolbrith, who had suggested Joaquin for a pen name (and also his costume of sombrero, cloak, boots and spurs) thought Miller might find fame abroad. Indeed he did, in London, as the six-foot, wild and woolly westerner who was said to bite the ankles of debutantes at dinner parties and smoke three cigars simultaneously. His *Songs of the Sierras*, published in England in 1871, won him wide popularity as a frontier poet.

Miller returned in the late 1880s, bought land in the Oakland Hills, and built his house, "The Hights," where he lived until his death at age seventy-two in 1913. On his hilltop he prophesied, philosophized, cultivated his eccentricities, planted thousands of trees and entertained friends like Ambrose Bierce, George Sterling and Jack London, plus throngs of admiring ladies. Generations of schoolchildren learned his poem, "Columbus," in which the great admiral declares, "Sail on! Sail on! Sail on! And on!"

When poet **YONE NOGUCHI**, father of sculptor Isamu Noguchi, was nineteen (in 1894) he was working on the San Francisco Japanese newspaper, *Soko Shimbun*, trying to eke out an existence and despairing of life in America. Someone suggested that he go see Joaquin Miller at the Hights because of Miller's interest in Japanese poetry. Noguchi went, and stayed four years. "What pleased me best, I confess," he wrote in his autobiography, *The Story of Yone Noguchi* (1915), "was Miller's manner in calling me 'Mr. Noguchi,' as it was the first occasion to hear myself so addressed since my arrival in California; hitherto I had been a Charley or a Frank according to the employer's fancy."

Noguchi and Miller collaborated on a book of poems, *Japan of Sword and Love*, published in Tokyo in 1905, where Noguchi returned and became a professor at the University of Tokyo.

Oriental poetry and Buddhism increasingly influenced San Francisco writers. Poet, critic and translator **KENNETH REXROTH** made distinguished translations, including *One Hundred Poems from the Japanese*, followed by *One Hundred Poems from the Chinese*. Rexroth was labeled the father of the Beat Generation, but long before the beat writers came to town, he had been holding soirees and poetry readings. Since the 1920s he had been at the center of the city's literary life and radical movements. A ruggedly good-looking man, who was a mountaineer, anarchist and autodidact with strong opinions, Rexroth declared, "Against the ruin of the world, there is only one defense—the creative act."As the exemplar of his philosophy, Rexroth was enormously productive. His many volumes of verse include *The Phoenix and the Tortoise* (1944), *Collected Shorter Poems* (1966) and *Longer Poems* (1968). *An Autobiographical Novel* deals with his youth; *The Alternative Society* is a collection of essays.

As San Francisco's "elder poetic statesman," Rexroth introduced, with high praise, the young Allen Ginsberg when Ginsberg read his long poem, "Howl," on that famous night that launched the beat movement at Six Gallery in 1955. Later Rexroth broke with the beats, calling their poetry "absolutely unmitigated crap." "They came to us late, from the slums of Greenwich Village, and they departed early, for the salons of millionairesses," he snarled, "comical bogies conjured up by the Luce publications."

It's hard to remember now that in 1953, when **LAWRENCE FERLINGHETTI** opened City Lights Bookstore in North Beach, the first all-paperback bookstore in the United States, most readers and publishers felt that paperbacks were not real books. But City Lights was an immediate success, and it still stands on the corner of Columbus and Broadway as a literary symbol and center of North Beach. Ferlinghetti, who earned a doctorate from the Sorbonne, brought the European traditions of paperbacks and independent bookstore publishing to America. Within two years of opening City Lights, he began to publish the Pocket Poet Series.

Born in Yonkers, New York, son of a French and Portuguese mother and an Italian immigrant father, Ferlinghetti came west in 1950, crossing the country by train. He took the ferry from Oakland to San Francisco and thrilled at his first sight of this white city rising on the hills. San Francisco was known as a

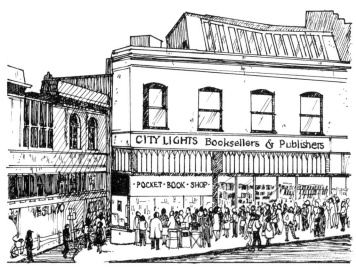

City Lights, North Beach

white city, he said, until businesses began to build black skyscrapers. He landed in North Beach, which was the Italian area, and there he has stayed, an enduring and endearing figure in the literary life of the city.

Ferlinghetti and Rexroth read their jazz poetry at North Beach nightclubs in the 1950s, and City Lights became the fulcrum for the beat writers, political radicals, and other avant-garde movements. One of the many framed mottoes hanging in his bookstore is: "Printer's Ink is the Great Explosive."

An early-movie buff, Ferlinghetti named his bookstore after the classic Charlie Chaplin film. The films of the 1920s, 1930s and 1940s, he notes nostalgically, are so innocent that even the villains are innocent. Now everyone is cynical, he laments; that appealing insouciance is lost.

A playful streak makes Ferlinghetti engaging when he reads his poetry, as he often does, both in the United States and Europe. While most of his work carries political messages, his more lyrical volume, *The Coney Island of the Mind* (1958), remains most popular worldwide. Among his other well-known collections of poetry are *An Eye on the World* (1976), *Open Eye, Open Heart* (1973) and *Landscapes of Living and Dying* (1979).

JACK KEROUAC first came west in 1947. In the next few years he made several frenzied trips back and forth from New York before he settled in as part of the local literary scene. From these travels, Kerouac captured a sense of the vastness of the continental United States and the larger-than-life characters who lived in some of its wide-open spaces. But, unlike Jack London's *The Road*, which was animated by a strong sense of outrage at the social injustice London encountered as a railroad tramp, Kerouac's quasi-autobiographical novel, *On the Road* (1957), was based on cross-country odysseys in speeding cars on a search for meaning in a crass world through experimental excesses of drugs, alcohol and sex.

On the Road became a literary landmark for the beat writers. Later, Kerouac, in a quieter phase of his continuing spiritual quest, studied first Mahayana Buddhism, then Zen, which San Francisco poet **GARY SNYDER** introduced him to. Buddhism informed his other most influential novel, *The Dharma Bums* (1958), in which Snyder appears as the character Japhy Ryder.

Born in Lowell, Massachusetts, in 1922 of devout Catholic, French-speaking parents from Quebec, Jack Kerouac didn't speak English until he was six. At Columbia University, when he was twenty-two, he met the eighteen-year-old Allen Ginsberg. Their mentor was the novelist William Burroughs, a bitter satirist of society and self-described drug addict whose best-known works are *The Naked Lunch* (1959) and *Junkie* (1964). Although a major influence on the beat writers, Burroughs was not part of the San Francisco literary scene.

In New York Kerouac also met **NEAL CASSADY,** already legendary for his frenetic energy, outrageous behavior and nonstop talk. Kerouac's distinctive style, which he called "spontaneous prose," was inspired by Cassady's monologues. Kerouac also coined the term "beat" (from *beatitude*) to denote seekers like himself. Later he repudiated it, writing in his introduction to *Lonesome Traveler* (1960) that he was "actually not 'Beat,' but [a] strange solitary crazy Catholic mystic."

Neal Cassady became Kerouac's great friend and traveling companion, whom Kerouac portrayed as Dean Moriarty in *On the Road*. Together they visited the West Coast in 1947. In 1952 Kerouac returned to San Francisco to live with Carolyn and Neal Cassady, who had settled there in 1948. Both Kerouac and Cassady were cult figures for the Beat Generation.

So was poet **ALLEN GINSBERG**, who put the Beat Generation and North Beach on the map. Born in New Jersey in 1926, Ginsberg migrated west after graduation from Columbia. In San Francisco he found a congenial atmosphere. Ginsberg carried a letter of introduction from William Carlos Williams, the "patron saint" of American poets, to Kenneth Rexroth. Rexroth suggested that Ginsberg organize a reading. Ginsberg advertised the event as a "Happy Apocalypse," later declaring: "Like this was the end of the McCarthy scene. The evening ended up with everybody absolutely radiant and happy, with talk and kissing and later on big happy orgies of poets."

Ginsberg's "Howl," a long indictment of modern corruption, gave vent to the frustrations of a youthful generation aching to burst the bonds of a conservative era. The San Francisco poetry renaissance was born, and media-savvy Ginsberg quickly became the guru of this counterculture.

National attention soon focused on North Beach when Ferlinghetti was arrested on obscenity charges for publishing *Howl and Other Poems*. After a long trial in the summer of 1957, Ferlinghetti was acquitted. But the case became a cause célèbre and gave the beat writers wide media coverage. It made Kerouac's *On the Road* a best-seller and enshrined City Lights as a bastion for artistic freedom.

Through the first heady years of national celebrity, when the coffeehouses and bars of North Beach were crowded with admirers and reporters hoping to snatch a word with them, Ginsberg and Kerouac remained friends. But Ginsberg, prolific, socially active, and with a genius for being in the limelight, found his star rising higher. Hard-drinking Kerouac supported the Vietnam War and disapproved of Ginsberg's pacifism and experiments with hallucinogenic drugs. Ginsberg coined the term "flower power" to describe the pacifist, mystic and romantic rebellion that carried the day in the sixties.

In 1973 Ginsberg won the National Book Award for *The Fall of America: Poems of These States*. But "Kaddish" (1961), a very personal lament for his dead mother, is often regarded as his best poem. *The Yate Letters* (1963) and *As Ever* (1977) are collections of his correspondence with his mentor William Burroughs and fellow-traveler Neal Cassady, respectively.

"So far as I am concerned this is the American Mediterranean," wrote **ALAN WATTS**, the leader of the Zen movement in the United States, and friend of Ferlinghetti, Kerouac and Ginsberg. Watts was born in England in 1913. In his autobiography, *In My Own Way* (1973), he wrote, "Here in San Francisco and Southern Marin . . . we have succeeded, more than anywhere else in the United States, in curbing the oppressive White Anglo-Saxon Protestant subculture of the nation." Telegraph Hill with its bohemian style of life reminded him of London's Chelsea, the Montmartre of Paris, and New York's Greenwich Village.

As a popularizer of Zen philosophy, particularly through *The Way of Zen* (1957), Watts became a rather unwilling guru for the beats. He criticized the movement's self-indulgences and excesses and wrote a severe essay, "Beat Zen, Square Zen and Zen," which Ferlinghetti's City Lights published as a pamphlet in 1958. But Watts and the beats became friends again. And he noted the deep and joyful communion that he and Ginsberg reached one night in a friend's apartment, chanting sutras, "Allen ringing the time with little Indian finger-cymbals."

"A universe which has manifested **GARY SNYDER** could never be called a failure," Watts once wrote. "When I am dead I would like to be able to say that he is carrying on everything I hold most dearly, though with a different style." After Watts died, Snyder dedicated a collection of his essays, *The Old Ways* (1977), to him.

Environmentalist and Buddhist, Zen poet Gary Snyder was born in San Francisco in 1930 but grew up in the Pacific Northwest, where he developed a love of animals, the outdoors and the pleasures of physical work. Educated at Reed College in Oregon, he returned to San Francisco in the 1950s, living in North Beach and becoming a significant figure in the beat movement. At Ginsberg's historic "Happy Apocalypse," Snyder read his environmentally conscious poem, "The Berry Farm."

Then he was off to Japan to study Zen for six years, returning again in time to be a host with Allen Ginsberg at the 1967 First Great Human Be-In in Golden Gate Park. A literary figure somewhat apart, Snyder now lives in the mountains of northern California, practicing the environmental and spiritual values of "bioregionalism" that his writing reflects. His *Turtle Island* (1974) won a Pulitzer Prize.

Although its tradition of bohemian-Buddhist-mystical-anarchist literary rebellion is long, the Telegraph Hill-North Beach neighborhood may be remembered best for those days when the Beat Generation held sway. Ferlinghetti called it a *quartier*, and as Simone de Beauvoir and Alan Watts noted, it recalls Montmartre, a neighborhood intimate to the "Lost Generation" of American writers in the 1920s. While pockets of literary life remain, the action of Telegraph Hill and North Beach has dispersed and the tourists have arrived. But a touch of *l'air* survives— in a whiff of lemon and spices, the sight of casually dressed groups of people in animated conversation over pasta and wine at marble-topped tables and of happy people with bundles of books coming out of City Lights Bookstore, still open seven days a week from 10 A.M. to midnight.

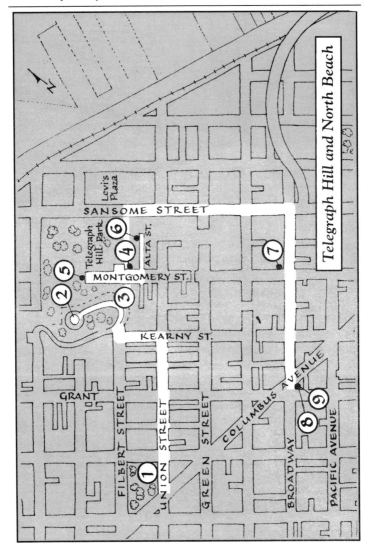

Walk 3: Telegraph Hill and North Beach

Begin at Washington Square on Union Street and Columbus Avenue.
End at Broadway and Columbus Avenue

From **Washington Square (1)** catch a No. 39 bus on Union Street
just west of Columbus Avenue for a three-minute ride to the top of
Telegraph Hill.

Visit **Coit Tower (2)** at the top of the hill, with its bold WPA
murals, including a panel of readers. Then walk back down the
roadway a short distance to **Filbert Stairs (3).**

Take the stairs down to Montgomery Street, cross to the retaining
wall and look right to the **1930s-style apartment building (4)** at
1360 on the lower level of Montgomery Street, a landmark made
famous in the film version of *The Maltese Falcon* by Dashiell
Hammett, starring Humphrey Bogart, and again in *Dark Passage*,
where Bogart calls on Lauren Bacall at this address.

Turn left on upper Montgomery Street and walk to the end, where
stands **Julius Castle (5),** a restaurant featured in many San Francisco
stories because of its setting on the hill and its spectacular view.

Turn sharp right onto lower Montgomery Street and walk up past
1360 to Alta, a short street typical of Telegraph Hill. Look down
Alta at the tiny, funky house at **No. 62 (6)** with ducks painted on
its side. Contemporary novelist Armistead Maupin once lived here.

Return on lower Montgomery Street to the Filbert Steps and continue
down. Where the wood steps end and the concrete ones begin is a
bench with a view—but not for those susceptible to giddiness if
they gaze down too long from great heights. Filbert Steps debouch
onto Sansome Street and Levi's Plaza, where there are ground-level
benches, an outdoor fountain and restaurants and snack bars.

With Levi's Plaza at your back, turn left and go south three blocks
on Sansome to Broadway. Turn right on Broadway past some sleazy
nightclubs to the large apartment building with entrances around

the corner at **1010 Montgomery Street (7),** where Allen Ginsburg lived in the early 1950s, when he wrote "Howl."

Continue on Broadway to Columbus Avenue. On the southwest corner of Broadway and Columbus is San Francisco's most famous bookstore, Lawrence Ferlinghetti's **City Lights Bookstore (8). Jack Kerouac Alley (9)** next door to City Lights leads to Chinese shops and markets.

North Beach abounds with coffee houses and ethnic restaurants on Columbus Avenue, on side streets and around Washington Square.

This walk is an easy hour, including a visit to Coit Tower, but excluding refreshment stops in Levi's Plaza and browsing in the City Lights Bookstore. If at the end of this walk you decide to take the Russian Hill walk, go south one block on Columbus Avenue to Pacific Avenue. Turn right on Pacific to the bus stop and take No. 83 up the hill through Chinatown. Get off at Jones. Walk one block north to Broadway.

Coit Tower, Telegraph Hill

Russian Hill

O cool, gray city of love!
— George Sterling

WRITERS AND ARTISTS have made their homes on the steep slopes of Russian Hill since the 1850s. And they still live here today despite the growth of high-priced, high-rise apartment buildings. Down wooded lanes and around cul-de-sacs are cottages and flats and Craftsman houses that can't be seen from the street. Here are hidden addresses accessible only by foot, and sudden, sheer views—in a city of superlative views—that take your breath away. On these windswept heights, San Francisco writers since Mark Twain and Bret Harte have gazed down from a vertical street or stairway, or from the bay window of a friend's studio or literary salon, on the glittering city spread below.

Journalist Ambrose Bierce, poet George Sterling and novelist Frank Norris lived here, as did Dashiell Hammett, Jack Kerouac and contemporary novelist **HERBERT GOLD**, author of *Fathers* (1967), *My Last Two Thousand Years* (1972) and *Family* (1981). For writers, a refuge on Russian Hill is still possible, and prized.

An assortment of authors, real and aspiring, have come and gone, but the longest-term literary resident and doyenne of Russian Hill was **INA COOLBRITH**. Gray-eyed and graceful, with a classic profile, Coolbrith was the friend and colleague of that bright, high-spirited group of young writers in the 1860s and 1870s that included Harte and Twain. There is still speculation about how intimate her friendships with them were. She, Bret Harte, and Charles Stoddard edited the influential literary magazine, the *Overland Monthly*, and were known as the "Golden Gate Trinity." Bret Harte wrote an affectionate limerick testifying to her influence:

> There is a poetic divinity,
> Number One of the Overland Trinity,
> Who uses the Muses
> Pretty Much as She Chooses,
> This dark-eyed young Sapphic divinity.

Coolbrith replied, referring to Bret as Francis (he was called Frank by his friends):

> There was a young writer named Francis,
> Who concocted such lurid romances
> That his publisher said
> You will strike this firm dead
> If you don't put a curb on your fancies.

In her poetry, considered among the best published in the *Overland Monthly*, there are hints of tragedy and lost love. But not until after her death was it known that Ina Coolbrith had been married briefly in Los Angeles to an insanely jealous man whom she fled to start a new life in San Francisco.

Born Josephine Smith in Illinois in 1842 (her uncle was the Mormon prophet, Joseph Smith), Coolbrith came west as a child with her family in a covered wagon train. Crossing the rugged Sierra Nevada mountains, the little girl of ten rode with the train's mulatto scout in front of his saddle, the first white child to enter California over the Beckwourth Pass.

When her literary talent was brightest, Ina Coolbrith harbored the dream of going east, perhaps as far as Europe, like her colleagues Twain, Harte, Joaquin Miller and others who were seeking fame and fortune. But then her widowed sister died, leaving two orphaned children for her to raise; her mother began to ail; and, before leaving for London, Miller deposited his half-Indian daughter with her.

To support her sudden household, Coolbrith found a job in the Oakland Public Library. There she had long talks with a ragged-looking lad named Jack London. She urged him to read Flaubert and Tolstoy and sent him home with armloads of books, some of them her own. Isadora Duncan was another young reader whom she encouraged. The famous dancer later learned that her father had a passionate, unrequited love for the magnetic Coolbrith, who became the muse for three generations of writers.

In 1915 the California state legislature appointed Coolbrith California's first poet laureate and awarded her a yearly stipend that lasted until her death in 1928 at the age of eighty-five.

Once Coolbrith had climbed up to her Russian Hill rooms with young men who became famous. In later life she sat in her house on the hill at Broadway and Taylor, a legendary figure wearing a white mantilla, receiving visitors and presiding over the meetings of the California Literary Society. Her criticism and encouragement were still sought after, but more and more the once-shining poet slipped into reverie. In *San Francisco's Literary Frontier* (1939), historian Franklin Walker records her saying:

> I was remembering yesterday what handsome men lived in San Francisco in the old days. It was hard to tell whether Frank Harte or Charlie Stoddard was the better-looking, and Joaquin Miller was quite striking with his curly brown hair. Mark Twain had an interesting face, but he was not as handsome as he was later. What a glorious time I used to have matching limericks with Frank . . . or joshing with Mark Twain, who was just a lanky red-headed journalist when he was working for the *Call*!

She was going to write a book about those early days, but all of her notes and letters were burned in the 1906 earthquake and fire, and she never did. But San Francisco did not forget Ina Coolbrith. Just below her house on Russian Hill, where she held her last salons, is a lovely terraced park bearing her name and a plaque dedicated to this first woman pioneer of San Francisco's literary life.

FRANK NORRIS lived briefly on Russian Hill in the 1890s. He had a great talent for storytelling and was maturing rapidly as a writer when peritonitis from a ruptured appendix caused his

Stairs to Macondray Lane, Russian Hill

death at thirty-two. His early novel, *Blix* (1899), was a story of young love set in Bohemian San Francisco. *McTeague*, also published in 1899, was a deeply serious novel about the self-destruction of a rapacious Polk Street dentist and his wife, Trina, whom Norris used as symbols of America's materialist society. This novel established Norris as one of America's first naturalistic writers. The gifted film director Eric von Stroheim turned *McTeague* into a silent film classic called *Greed*. Shot on the streets of San Francisco in 1923, it is a superb visual record of the city in the early part of the century.

Of Norris's projected trilogy, *Epic of the Wheat*, depicting the effects of economic forces on people, only *The Octopus* (1901) was completed. It was based on the actual struggle of California ranchers against the Southern Pacific Railroad, the octopus of the title. *The Pit* (1902), set around the Chicago wheat exchange, was published, uncorrected, after his death. A great talent was lost when this handsome young man died.

"I'm a-gunning for stories," Frank Norris wrote in the 1890s. "Things can happen in San Francisco." It was, he said, a story city, and he wrote about it feverishly.

About the same time, poet **GEORGE STERLING** was penning his rhymed meters. When *Testimony of the Suns* was published in 1903, Ambrose Bierce, long-time denizen of Russian Hill, told him, "You shall be the poet of the skies, the prophet of the sun." Sterling is not much read now, but on Russian Hill in the quiet, shaded George Sterling Glade, his lines to San Francisco are cast in bronze:

> Tho the dark be cold and blind
> Yet her sea fog's touch is kind.
> And her mightier caress
> Is joy and pain thereof!
> And great is thy tenderness
> O cool, gray city of love!

George Sterling's place in San Francisco's literary history is assured by his association with other writers, particularly Jack London, all of whose books Sterling edited and proofed. They were close friends, hiking, fishing, drinking and carousing together.

As Ferlinghetti wrote in his *Literary San Francisco* (co-authored with Nancy Peters), Sterling was a legend in his own time: "Profligate, charming, a lyric personality, a catalyst for renewal of literary activity in the Bay Area." Sterling's celebrated verse play of 1907, *The Triumph of Bohemia*, was produced by the Bohemian Club in the days when the club truly was made up of bohemians. Later his life went into decline, he drank more and more, and in 1926, he committed suicide in his room at the Bohemian Club.

Not until she wrote her own books, *Heartbeat* (1976) and *Off the Road: My Years with Cassady, Kerouac, and Ginsberg* (1990), was much known about **CAROLYN CASSADY** other than by Beat Generation aficionados. But she was den mother for them all.

In a very small, brown-shingle house on a singularly unromantic side street on Russian Hill, Carolyn kept house for Cassady and Kerouac. While Neal was writing his rambling works (finally published in 1971 by City Lights as *The First Third & Other Writings*) and Jack was revising *On the Road* to apotheosize Cassady as the beat idol, the beautiful, blonde Carolyn cooked, cleaned and served as sexual partner for both men. Their *ménage à trois* was a model for the macho avant-garde of the 1950s. Neal was the avatar of the Beat Generation and Jack the chronicler. Carolyn was thrilled to have a role in their life on Russell Street:

> I began a season singing days and nights, I was *part* of all they did now and I felt like the star of the show. Besides, I felt I was a real contributor for once. My house work and baby care had a *purpose*; it was needed and appreciated. I was functioning as a female, and my men were men. . . . .I served whichever one was in residence according to their individual requirements. If

they were both home at once, Neal usually slept and Jack wrote. Jack tried to go out and leave the real husband and wife alone if Neal was up and about.

The marriage in 1948 of Carolyn Robinson, a well-brought-up Bennington College scholarship graduate, and Neal Cassady, the abandoned kid who became a car thief and hustler, was the ultimate attraction of opposites. They lived in San Francisco for five years before moving down the peninsula to San Jose and eventually Los Gatos. While Cassady was in and out of jail and careening around the country with his cohorts in search of drugs, sex, and ever more bizarre excitement, Carolyn raised their three children. Eventually they divorced. Neal died in 1968, and Carolyn kept on painting and writing, and belatedly putting together her own life. Determined to tell her story, she finally succeeded with what one reviewer of *Off the Road* declared was not a "rehash" but "a great book, as well as a wonderful autobiography."

Today's San Francisco scene is, of course, quite different, and there is no more hip chronicler of its rapid change than **ARMISTEAD MAUPIN**. A modern-day Trollope, Maupin has caught the city's beat with his funny, sad, preposterous and true tales of San Francisco types. Walk downhill from Ina Coolbrith Park on Taylor Street and climb the wooden stairs to secluded Macondray Lane, where (most readers agree) Maupin's lovable, eccentric Mrs. Madrigal has her small apartment building. Down this wooded lane, it's easy to imagine her in her leafy bower dispensing gentle advice and homegrown marijuana to her favorite renters, gay Michael and straight Mary Ann.

Maupin's novels, beginning with *Tales of the City*, have become best-sellers. Like Mrs. Madrigal, Michael and Mary Ann, everybody's hooked on the cool, gray city of love.

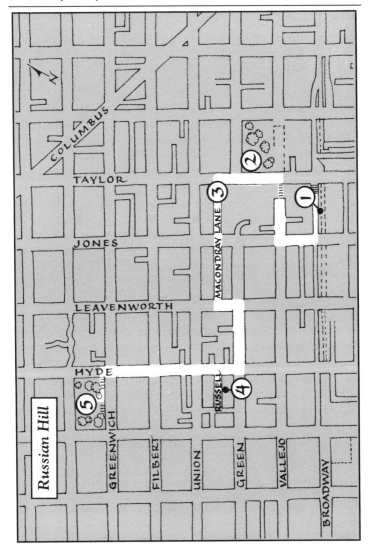

Walk 4: Russian Hill

Begin at Broadway and Jones.
End at Hyde and Greenwich.

At Broadway and Jones, walk a half block east on Broadway to where it dead-ends at a retaining wall with built-in seats on the far side at either end. The view of the east bay and the Bay Bridge is magnificent. On your right at **No. 1067 (1)** is the home of California's first poet laureate and mentor to Jack London, Ina Coolbrith.

Return to Jones. Turn right and walk north on Jones one block, keeping to the right up a short hill past a "No Through Street" sign. Follow the street around to its dead end at the top of the hill for an even more spectacular panoramic view. To the right of the balustrade, take the nearly hidden stairway down to Taylor Street. Directly across Taylor is **Ina Coolbrith Park (2).**

Return to the stairway side of Taylor. With the park behind you, turn right and go north downhill on Taylor until you reach a set of wooden stairs leading up to **Macondray Lane (3),** the most likely location of fictional Barbary Lane and the small apartment house of Armistead Maupin's eccentric, beloved Mrs. Madrigal and her "children" in his best-selling *Tales of the City* series of novels.

You can walk to the end of the wooded portion of Macondray Lane and return to Broadway and Jones, making this a thirty- to forty-five-minute walk.

Or you can continue to the end of Macondray Lane and turn left on Leavenworth one block to Green. Then turn right on Green one block downhill to Hyde. Cross to the west side of Hyde and turn right. A half block north on Hyde is Russell, a short, dead-end street. **No. 29 Russell (4)** was the home of Carolyn and Neal Cassady, and Jack Kerouac lived with them here in a *ménage à trois*.

Continue uphill on Hyde (or catch a cable car) to Greenwich. At Greenwich, turn left up a short flight of stairs past the Alice Marble Tennis Courts. (Alice Marble was a world-class tennis player who claimed to have been a spy for the United States in World War II.) Continue across the top of the hill and then down a few stairs. At the first landing, turn right into **George Sterling Glade (5)**. The glade has the quiet air of an Old World garden with its formal row of benches and pollarded trees and, in front of a colored tile wall, its pillar with a plaque commemorating the poet.

Return to Hyde and Greenwich.

Total walking time is approximately one hour.

Haight-Ashbury and Golden Gate Park

San Francisco was in my blood and bones. I knew it as
a very small child and a little later as a whistling boy.
— *William Saroyan*

FOR A LONG TIME before Haight-Ashbury became an international synonym for the hippie counterculture, it was a quiet, genteel neighborhood of large Victorian houses. One of many splendid examples still stands a block off Haight and a few streets down from Ashbury. This house, at 1990 Page Street, with its beautiful bow window, pillared porch, fanlights, cornices and dormer, all decorated with delicate swags and bows, testifies to the exuberance of the late 1800s, when it was built. It was once owned by novelist **KATHLEEN NORRIS**, "America's favorite writer" of the 1920s (she wrote seventy-five books in her long career), who, for the twenty years that she lived in New York, had a caretaker look after it.

Norris lived briefly in the old Montgomery Block, or "Monkey Block," in the opening years of the 1900s. Her novel, *Mother*, published in 1911, set her unvarying tone of wholesome family comedy and tragedy.

When Norris returned to the Bay Area after achieving fame in the East, she found San Francisco "still as surprising, as fascinating, as original as ever she was . . . the gray silhouette of her hills, shingled with roofs and roofs and roofs . . . the gray fog circling and fuming softly over it all, and the gulls flying and crying. The Angelus bells in a long chord" struck her heart as a "Welcome home!"

Kathleen Norris's sentimental heart would have been saddened to see how, particularly from the 1940s on, the old neighborhood steadily declined, and she would have been horrified at the psychedelic scene in the Haight in the 1960s and 1970s. But, happily, hers and other fine old Victorian houses in the neighborhood, many of which were once occupied by communes or cut up as rooming houses, are now being restored to their original elegance.

"It was at 348 Carl Street twenty years ago on this day, October 13 [1934] that I opened a package from Random House and saw a copy of my first book," wrote **WILLIAM SAROYAN**. The book was *The Daring Young Man on the Flying Trapeze*, and with its publication, the ebullient young Saroyan was launched on his long career as a short-story writer, playwright and novelist. He remembered that it was "a hell of a moment."

> I was so excited I couldn't roll a Bull Durham cigarette. After three tries I finally made it, and began to inhale and exhale a little madly as I examined the preposterous and very nearly unbelievable object of art and merchandise. What a book, what a cover, what a title page, what words, what a photograph—now just watch the women swarm around. For a young writer *does* write in order to expect pretty women to swarm around. I also meant to revolutionize American writing.

While he didn't exactly revolutionize writing in America, Saroyan contributed his own exuberant affirmation of the American dream in a steady flow of short stories, plays and novels. Many, like his humorous and appealing *My Name Is Aram* (1940), about an Armenian boy growing up in Fresno, are based on his own life.

Saroyan loved offbeat personalities, in whom he always saw the best. His melding of those he knew into characters in his Pulitzer Prize-winning play, *The Time of Your Life* (1939), produced a heartwarming story set in a saloon like his own favorite, Izzy Gomez's.

"The San Francisco of the late thirties was Saroyan's town," columnist Herb Caen wrote. "He was buoyantly everywhere: prowling the waterfront . . . darting into Opera Alley to bet at his favorite book-maker's, drinking champagne in Sally Stanford's parlor [Stanford was a well-known madame], being lionized by lush Nob Hill society ladies, philosophizing loudly and often brilliantly over the grappa at Izzy Gomez's." The city was smaller then, Caen remembered, and "warmer, more sentimental, and Saroyan captured its flavor with great precision" in *The Time of Your Life*.

Saroyan once recounted a conversation he had as a youngster with his older brother Henry. Henry had been taken with his class to the Oakland hilltop home of Joaquin Miller, whose poem "Columbus" the schoolchildren had learned to recite. When Saroyan asked his brother about the famous man, Henry said, "He's very old, has a long beard, [and] lies on a couch. He said, 'Now, boys, I've planted a thousand eucalyptus trees all over these Oakland hills, and I want you to plant trees wherever you go, too.'"

It was a worthy command. But Saroyan commented sarcastically, "The man was such a nice phoney." He may have been thinking of Joaquin Miller's oft-repeated claim, "I cry aloud from my mountain top, as a seer." Or his penchant for such tricks as evoking rain from a cloudless sky with bogus Indian chants: unfailingly a shower fell from a hidden sprinkler tipped from his roof by his assistant, Yone Noguchi.

The message in Saroyan's writing is, according to Herb Caen: "Peace is better than war, love is better than hate and the world is infinitely sad and mad."

KAY BOYLE would agree emphatically with that sentiment. Novelist, short-story writer and poet, Boyle had been one of the avant-garde American expatriate writers in Paris in the 1920s and 1930s. But from 1963 until 1979, when she was in her sixties and seventies and the Haight was in its hippie period, Kay Boyle lived about six blocks from the corner of Haight and Ashbury. And for seventeen years her four-story Victorian house at 419 Frederick Street was a radical political hub. Upstairs, she wrote in bed with her typewriter on her knees; downstairs, she met with political activists; and out on the street, she marched in protest against the Vietnam War.

A striking woman, always immaculately groomed, Boyle is driven by what she calls her "crusading spirit." While her work is noted for its polish and range (the poet William Carlos Williams was one of her earliest mentors), it has steadily become more political. Her *Testament for My Students, 1968–1969* and *The Long Walk at San Francisco State* (1970) (she taught at the university) express her solidarity with the youthful rebellion against conformity that swirled around her.

Boyle's passionate involvement in the issues of the day is reflected in her novel *The Underground Woman* (1975). It tells the story of a woman much like herself who is jailed for anti-Vietnam War protests and whose daughter, with fellow members of a cult, takes over her home. In fact, Boyle was jailed twice for her protests. And two of her six children joined a cult led by Mel Lyman, an admirer of mass-murderer Charles Manson. One fall morning in 1970, commune members stormed Boyle's home on Frederick Street.

"We are going to have that house if we have to burn it to the ground," her daughter's husband told her. In a desperate maneuver, she deeded the house to her neighbor for $1 and he evicted the commune.

Such a searing experience might have soured many on youth in general, but not Kay Boyle. While she mourns the loss of her daughter (her son eventually split from the cult), her faith in youthful idealism has not dimmed. She once picketed a landlord in the Haight who had raised his rents excessively, causing her neighbors to suggest a "Kay Boyle for President" movement. Boyle no longer lives on Frederick Street, but while she was there, her house was crowded with kindred spirits, working for their vision of a better world.

The 1960s counterculture dream of changing the world reached its apotheosis at the Human Be-In Gathering of the Tribes on the polo fields of Golden Gate Park, January 14, 1967. Early that morning, Allen Ginsberg and Gary Snyder performed an ancient Hindu bene-diction rite by chanting prescribed prayers as they circumambulated the grassy fields where the gathering would be held. This was to assure the Human Be-In the status of a religious pilgrimage, or *mela*.

And what a *mela* it was! Thousands of people congregated on the green to usher in a new age. The hip stores on Haight Street closed so that everyone could attend. Incense mingled with the aroma of marijuana, and people mellowed out or tripped on LSD. Bells, cymbals, tambourines, feathers and fur were everywhere. The Hell's Angels motorcyclists kept order, and on the stage bands like

Kay Boyle's house, Haight-Ashbury

the Jefferson Airplane and the Grateful Dead rotated. When the sun began to set, Gary Snyder blew on a conch shell, Allen Ginsberg led a chant, and the age of love, peace and harmony was ushered in.

Following the Human Be-In came the 1967 Summer of Love, when literally thousands of young people from across the country poured into Haight-Ashbury, hoping to be a part of the new age. The streets were jammed. Drug dealers hawked their wares, crying "Acid, speed, lids?" Long-haired, bearded youths sat in front of shops beating their bongo drums, and Hell's Angels motorcyclists roared up Haight Street. And the Gray Line Bus Company offered a San Francisco Haight-Ashbury "Hippie Hop" tour.

But it was **KEN KESEY** who had already taken the show on the road in 1964 with his band of itinerant hippies called the Merry Pranksters. One of the last of the Beat Generation, the indefatigable Neal Cassady, joined the Pranksters and was on hand to help Kesey develop the psychedelic "happenings" with their "acid tests" that popularized the use of LSD. Cassady also drove the Merry Pranksters' bus painted in Day-Glo and bearing the destination, "Further." Kesey's two novels, *One Flew over the Cuckoo's Nest* (1962), based on his experiences as a guinea pig for drug testing in a Palo Alto, California, veterans' hospital, and *Sometimes a Great Notion* (1964), centering on a brotherly feud in an Oregon lumber town, secured his reputation as a literary spokesman for the 1960s. And Tom Wolfe preserved the story of the Merry Pranksters (who frolicked in San Francisco) in his *The Electric Kool-Aid Acid Test* (1968).

RICHARD BRAUTIGAN came of age during the Haight-Ashbury period and was a literary idol of the 1960s and 1970s. Like Ken

Kesey, he served as a link between the beats and the hippies. His short "novel" composed of comic, surrealistic sketches, *Trout Fishing in America* (1967), sold more than two million copies. It and his other early novels, *A Confederate General from Big Sur* (1965) and *In Watermelon Sugar* (1968) were required reading for the hip generation.

But the Haight-Ashbury culture did not produce any literary giants. Rather, it wound down to a depressing end, as Joan Didion describes in "Slouching toward Bethlehem." By 1969 the Haight was suffering from a major heroin epidemic. The neighborhood hit rock bottom. Then the exponents of drug guru Timothy Leary's creed, "Tune in, turn on, drop out," began to disperse. Ken Kesey went back to Oregon to run a dairy farm. His Pranksters and others drifted north away from the city, Richard Brautigan to Montana, where he committed suicide at the age of forty-nine.

By the 1980s much of the philosophy and trappings of the counterculture had been absorbed into mainstream America. And the Haight-Ashbury began to pull itself together again. Boarded-up stores on Haight Street reopened. All over the neighborhood the old Victorian houses and ornamented commercial buildings began to be refurbished, their scrollwork and carvings repainted with loving care. And while a few bongo drummers, barefoot panhandlers, and black-leather-jacketed bikers perpetuate the memory of the hippie era, the Haight is eminently livable once again, safe, funky, and fun. And maybe now, in one of the bow- window alcoves, a new young writer is keying into a lap-top computer the latest story of a western movement. San Francisco is still where it happens.

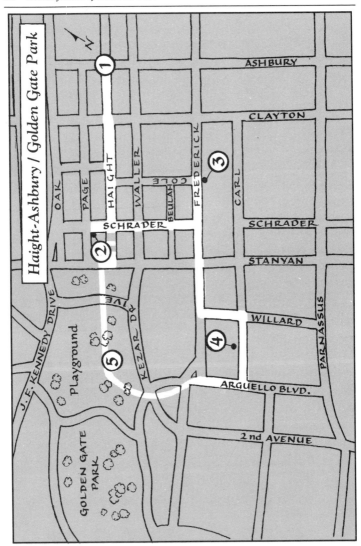

Haight-Ashbury / Golden Gate Park

Walk 5: Haight-Ashbury and Golden Gate Park

Begin at Haight and Ashbury. End at Haight and Stanyan.

This walk is more enjoyable in the morning before the streets are crowded and motorcyclists gather at the end of Haight across Stanyan on the edge of Golden Gate Park.

Alternative ways to see the area are to rent rollerskates or skateboards along Haight, or bikes or mopeds along Stanyan.

From the famous corner at **Haight and Ashbury (1),** walk west along Haight. Turn right on Schrader to Page. **No. 901 Page (2),** on the southwest corner of Schrader and Page, was 1920s novelist Kathleen Norris's house; she had a caretaker look after it for twenty years while she lived in New York.

Return on Schrader, crossing Haight. Turn left on Frederick to **419 Frederick (3),** contemporary novelist and social activist Kay Boyle's former home, nearly hidden by trees.

Return along Frederick, crossing Schrader and Stanyan. Turn left up one short, steep hill on Willard, then right on Carl. **348 Carl (4)** was the residence of playwright, poet and novelist William Saroyan from 1932 until 1939.

Turn right on Arguello Boulevard. Take the footpath across the field to cross Kezar Drive at the stoplight. Immediately inside Golden Gate Park, step behind an iron fence on your right. Follow the path past the children's playground to the beautiful large, grassy field edged at the opposite side by **"Hippie Hill" (5)**—an area made famous when it was thick with flower children in the 1960s and 1970s. Benches here are perfect for people watching.

Continue east along the path, crossing busy Kezar Drive (not marked) at the first crosswalk. Take the footpath through a green strip to Stanyan and then turn left on Haight.

This walk takes less than an hour, exclusive of bookstore browsing, shopping, or snack or meal stops along Haight, or picnicking in Golden Gate Park.

The John Muir House, Martinez, California

Across the Bay

Three writers' homes that are preserved and open to the public are situated across the Golden Gate Bridge or the Bay Bridge from San Francisco. Those of **JOHN MUIR** and **EUGENE O'NEILL** can be visited in a long half-day. But a trip to **JACK LONDON**'s ranch in the Jack London State Historic Park near Glen Ellen, Sonoma County, requires a full day.

A shorter trip can be made to the little house that **JOAQUIN MILLER** called home. It is in Oakland and stands boarded up in a bed of weeds at the corner of Joaquin Miller Road and Sanborn Drive at one of the entrances to the Joaquin Miller Park. The seventy acres that "the poet of the Sierras" bought in 1880 is now incorporated into the five-hundred-acre park named in his honor. At the ranger station on Sanborn Drive is a small exhibit, with photographs of Miller and a few excerpts from his works. Well-marked trails traverse the park, which is a favorite for runners and joggers.

JOHN MUIR NATIONAL HISTORIC SITE, 4202 Alhambra Avenue, Martinez, CA 94553, 415-228-8860. Open Wednesday through Sunday, 10:00 A.M. to 4:30 P.M. Admission, $1.00; free to those under seventeen and and over sixty-one. From San Francisco, Martinez is about an hour's drive northeast via Interstate 80, then Highway 4.

The impassioned writings of naturalist John Muir (1838-1914) made him the leader of the early wilderness conservation movement. He founded the Sierra Club and served as president from 1892 until his death in 1914. Muir conveyed his poetic appreciation of nature with great stylistic effect, and he helped preserve many wilderness areas in the West, including his beloved Yosemite Valley.

A brilliant loner, with a passion for forests and glaciers, Muir traveled widely, whenever possible by foot. In 1867 when he was twenty-five he walked from Indiana to the Gulf of Mexico. His journal of the trip was edited posthumously as *A Thousand Mile Walk to the Gulf* (1916). He was a striking figure, tall and lean, with handsome features, a wild beard and piercing eyes. One of his more famous exploits was climbing a great Douglas fir tree on a mountaintop in the middle of a violent lightning storm to experience what the tree felt. Clinging to the topmost branches, he swayed wildly with the tree, howling in ecstasy. "The King tree and I," he wrote, "have sworn eternal love."

Other influential books by John Muir include *The Mountains of California* (1894), *My First Summer in the Sierra* (1911), *The Yosemite* (1912), and *Travels in Alaska* (1915).

Difficult as it was for Muir to come inside from the wilderness he loved, he finally married and lived with his wife and family in this seventeen-room Victorian house for the last twenty-four years of his life. Here he made enough money from his surrounding 2,600-acre ranch to support his travels and writings. The well-furnished house is full of wonderful memorabilia. His study, or "scribble den," contains his desk and that of his daughter, who typed his books for him. Despairing of his piles of papers and notes all over the floor and of his constant revising, she placed a box beside her typewriter. There, she instructed her father, he was to place the manuscript ready for her to type—rolled up and tied with a red ribbon.

Only 8.8 acres of the ranch are preserved in this historic site, and traffic on the John Muir Parkway (a singularly inappropriate memorial) roars by just below the house. But you can turn your back on the highway and stroll through the remaining orchards, where gardeners harvest the fruit and place it in boxes behind the Visitor Center for guests to help themselves—as John Muir would have wished.

Tao House at the **EUGENE O'NEILL NATIONAL HISTORIC SITE,**
P.O. Box 280, Danville, CA 94553. Open Wednesday through
Sunday at 10:00 A.M. and 12:30 P.M. It is about an hour's drive west
from San Francisco on Highway 24, then south on Interstate 680
to Danville. Transportation from downtown Danville. Tours by
reservations only. Call 415-838-0249.

Tao House, on the crest of a golden hill outside of Danville,
was the last home of America's first great playwright, Eugene O'-
Neill (1888–1953). Here he wrote his final and best plays, including *The Iceman Cometh*, *Long Day's Journey into Night*, and *A Moon
for the Misbegotten*. O'Neill was awarded the Pulitzer Prize four
times, and in 1936 he won the Nobel Prize for literature. That
same year O'Neill and his wife, Carlotta, moved to California in
search of the privacy he craved and a place where they could put
down roots. They fell in love with the gentle, rolling hills of the
East Bay area and, after the sudden windfall from the Nobel
Prize, were able to buy one hundred fifty acres of a former ranch.
The next year they built Tao House.

"I will always be a stranger who never feels at home," O'Neill
once wrote, but Tao House changed that feeling. Designed to suit
the O'Neills' needs exactly, the house has some curious features. In
order to write, O'Neill needed complete quiet, so his study is tucked
away at the far end of the house, accessible only by a passageway
with three doors from his bedroom through his wardrobe, much like
the interior of a ship. The study has wood paneling and a beamed
ceiling, and the only adornment on the wall is a copy of O'Neill's
seaman's certificate of discharge.

Like Jack London, O'Neill treasured memories of sea voyages
made when he was an adventurous youth, and he drew upon these
experiences in his writing. Also like London, when he had achieved
fame and money he bought a California ranch, raised chickens and
planted trees.

The wide view of rolling hills that O'Neill so loved is nearly the same as it was when he lived there. The remaining thirteen acres of his property is protected from development on three sides by the East Bay Regional Park System. The National Park Service, which conducts tours through the house and grounds, is restoring them to their original state and acquiring Chinese rugs and antiques similar to those owned by the O'Neills. Many items here actually belonged to the O'Neills, such as the teakwood dog bed with its satin sheets, pillow and blanket for their beloved and pampered Dalmation, "Blemie."

Tao House's ceilings are painted blue like the heavens and its doors Chinese red for good luck. But auspicious as the atmosphere was in O'Neill's isolated retreat, it could not ward off the Parkinson's disease that slowly made it impossible for him to write. Ultimately this lovely spot became a place of heartbreak as O'Neill's disease progressed and labor shortages caused by World War II made it increasingly difficult to hire help. Photographs of family and friends fill out the story—including some of his daughter, Oona, who married Charlie Chaplin against her father's strong objections.

The only access to Tao House is by way of a private road, so a Park Service van meets visitors in downtown Danville for the seven-minute ride up the hill.

JACK LONDON STATE HISTORIC PARK, 2400 London Ranch Road, Glen Ellen, CA 95442, 707-938-5216. The eight-hundred-acre park with twenty miles of trails is open daily 8 A.M. until the closing time posted at the entrance station. The museum in the House of Happy Walls is open 10 A.M. to 5 P.M. daily except Thanksgiving, Christmas and New Year's Day. Admission $5 per vehicle. For information on guided horseback rides through the park, call Sonoma Cattle Co., 707-996-8566. From San Francisco, Jack London State Park is about an hour's drive north on Interstate

101, then east and south on Highway 12 to Glen Ellen and London Ranch Road.

Jack London (1876–1916) was one of the most romantic figures of his day and one of the most popular American writers of all time. His short stories and novels have been translated into dozens of languages. Handsome, adventurous, and enormously energetic, he had an action-packed life that culminated in his purchase and development of his beloved Beauty Ranch in the Sonoma orchard and wine country. He called himself a "sailor on horseback" and wrote:

> I ride over my beautiful ranch. Between my legs is a beautiful horse. The air is wine. The grapes on a score of rolling hills are red with autumn flame. Across the Sonoma Mountain, wisps of sea fog are stealing. The afternoon smolders in the drowsy sky. I have everything to make me glad I am alive.

Strolling along the Jack London Park trails, it is easy to feel the magic that drew London to Sonoma County in 1911: "When I first came here, tired of cities and people, I settled down on a little farm—130 acres of the most beautiful, primitive land to be found in California."

Jack London had grown up on the Oakland waterfront. At age fourteen he worked in a cannery. At sixteen he became an oyster pirate, then switched to the side of the law and joined the fish patrol in San Francisco Bay. At seventeen he went to sea on a sealing schooner. By eighteen he had turned hobo, riding the rails across America. But he wanted to be a writer and to escape the brutal physical labor of his youth. So in marathon twenty-hour days he read voraciously and wrote prolifically. His seventh novel, *The Call of the Wild*, brought him instant celebrity. When he built the house of his dreams, he named it Wolf House after that story about the sled dog, Buck, whose primitive instincts surface in the wild and who escapes from civilization to become the leader of a wolf pack.

In 1911 Jack and his second wife, Charmain, began planning their four-story, twenty-six-room dream house, built of stone and redwood to last a thousand years. On August 22, 1913, the night before they were to move their custom-built furniture into the house, they were awakened at 2 A.M. Wolf House was on fire! It burned to the ground, leaving nothing but a stone skeleton rising amid the towering redwoods. A suspicion of arson (which was never proved) deeply depressed London. He had poured all his money into building Wolf House as well as into projects to make Beauty Ranch a model working farm. He was seriously in debt. He had to keep writing, which he did in the cottage where he and Charmain lived and where he died three years later from the ravages of alcohol, ill health and an overdose of morphine.

The cottage, with its glassed-in porch where London wrote, is still standing, as are the evocative ruins of the great Wolf House.

After Jack died, Charmain built the House of Happy Walls, a smaller stone house, where she lived until her death in 1955. It is now a museum full of London memorabilia from his writing life and extensive travels. You can press a button and see a poignant snatch of film showing Jack on a horse, feeding his pigs, driving a fertilizer spreader, posing with Charmain, and waving goodbye. It was taken six days before he died.

Jack London's ashes are buried under the trees, marked only by a large boulder on a knoll next to the wooden crosses of two pioneer children.

A walk to all of these ranch sites, as well as farm buildings such as the "pig palace," London's uniquely designed piggery with a "suite" for each pig, and the "manure pit" built by Italian stonemasons, can be done easily in about two hours.

Another hour and a half or so is needed to do a roundtrip hike on the fairly strenuous uphill trail to the five-acre lake that London created. He and Charmain often entertained their guests here.

Picnic tables and barbecue facilities are available in the park. Glen Ellen and the surrounding area offer a wide variety of restaurants and wineries.

Further Reading

Cassady, Carolyn. *Off the Road: My Years with Cassady, Kerouac and Ginsberg*. New York: W. Morrow, 1990.

Clark, Tom. *Jack Kerouac: A Biography*. New York: Paragon House, 1990.

Ferlinghetti, Lawrence, and Nancy J. Peters. *Literary San Francisco: A Pictorial History*, San Francisco: City Lights Books/Harper & Row, 1980.

Halper, Jon. *Gary Snyder: Dimensions of a Life*. San Francisco: Sierra Club Books, 1991.

Hamalian, Linda. *The Force behind the San Francisco Renaissance: A Life of Kenneth Rexroth*. New York: Norton, 1991.

Johnson, Diane. *Dashiell Hammett, A Life*. New York: Random House, 1983.

Lee, Lawrence. *Saroyan: A Biography*. New York: Paragon House, 1988.

Leider, Emily Wortis. *California's Daughter: Gertrude Atherton and Her Times*. Stanford, Calif.: Stanford University Press, 1991.

Lennon, Nigey. *The Sagebrush Bohemian: Mark Twain in California*. New York: Paragon House, 1990.

Michaels, Leonard, David Reid and Raquel Scherr, editors. *West of the West: Imagining California, An Anthology*. New York: HarperPerennial, 1990.

Miles, Barry. *Ginsberg: A Biography*. New York: HarperPerennial, 1990.

Miller, John. *San Francisco Stories: Great Writers on the City*. San Francisco: Chronicle Books, 1990.

Perry, Charles. *The Haight-Ashbury: A History*. New York: Vintage Books, 1985.

Silesky, Barry. *Ferlinghetti: The Artist in His Time*. New York: Warner Books, 1990.

Spanier, Sandra Whipple. *Kay Boyle: Artist and Activist*. New York: Paragon House, 1988.

Stewart, George R. *Bret Harte, Argonaut and Exile*. New York: AMS Press, 1979.

Stone, Irving. *Irving Stone's Jack London, His Life, Sailor on Horseback (a Biography) and 28 Selected Jack London Short Stories*. Garden City, NY: Doubleday, 1977.

Turner, Frederick W. *John Muir in His Time and Ours*. San Francisco: Sierra Club Books, 1985.

Twain, Mark. *Roughing It*. New York: Penguin, 1981.

Wolfe, Tom. *The Electric Kool-Aid Acid Test*. New York: Bantam Books, 1969.

Index